O. M. EDV
AND THE WE

G000124159

JOHN EVANS

Illustrated by Malcolm Stokes

DREF WEN

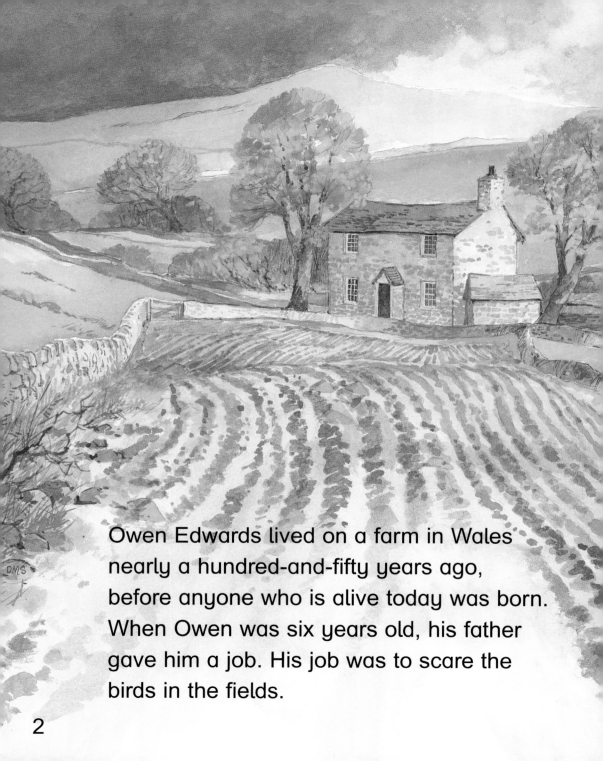

Owen Edwards lived on a farm in Wales
nearly a hundred-and-fifty years ago,
before anyone who is alive today was born.
When Owen was six years old, his father
gave him a job. His job was to scare the
birds in the fields.

2

His father had made him a special rattle
to make a noise, so that the birds would
fly away. Owen shouted "Ewch i ffwrdd!"
as well to frighten the birds.

All Owen's friends spoke Welsh. No-one
could really speak English very well.
When Owen and his friends played,
they talked in Welsh.

When Owen and his family sat at the
table to eat their food, they spoke in Welsh.

When Owen went to chapel every
Sunday, he sang hymns in Welsh and
said prayers in Welsh. But when Owen
went to school, he had to speak in English.

6

Owen did not like school. The school-teacher said, "I do not want to hear anyone speaking in Welsh, or you will be punished!"

cat
bat
fat
mat
sat
rat

Owen tried to speak in English, but he
found it hard. So did his friends,
especially when they were playing
in the school yard.

9

The teacher listened carefully in case
she heard some Welsh.
She heard Gwilym speaking Welsh.

She grabbed him by the collar and
shouted loudly at him, "You will now wear
the Welsh Not around your neck. Listen
carefully until you hear someone else
speak Welsh. Then pass the Welsh Not
to him."

11

Owen shouted in Welsh to his friend.
Gwilym passed the Welsh Not to him.
Owen wore it all day. He heard many
children speaking Welsh, but he would
not pass on the Welsh Not.

At the end of the day, Owen stood at the teacher's desk. The teacher said, "Hold out your hand, you naughty boy!" Owen did as he was told. Then the teacher hit him six times with her cane. Owen cried all the way home.

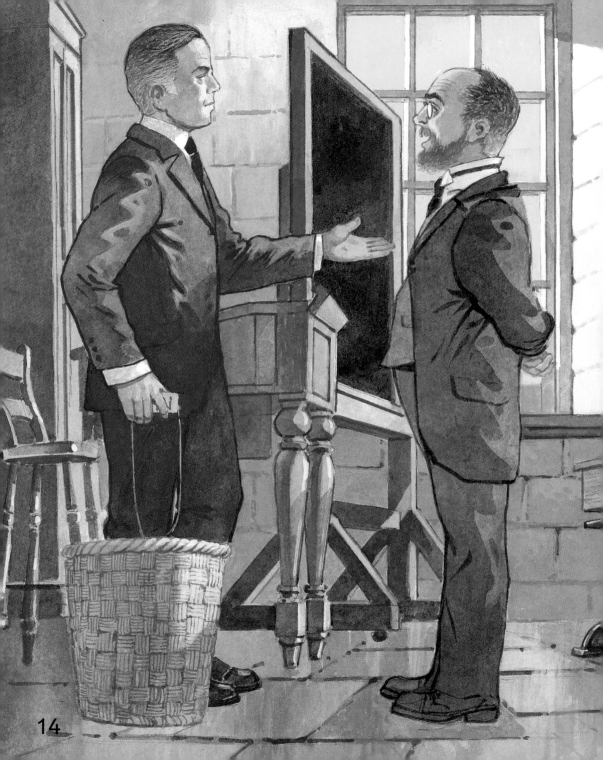

14

When Owen grew up, he became a school inspector. He inspected all the schools in Wales to make sure that the teachers were doing their work properly. He did not like the Welsh Not. He made all the teachers stop using it.
He said it was very important for children to learn English, but it was just as important for them to speak Welsh.

INDEX